THIS WORKBOOK BELONGS TO:

_____

ImpactArise Publishing

TEEN BIBLE STUDY WORKBOOK
POWER: EDITION

AN ARISE TO GROW TEEN RESOURCE BY

REGINE JEAN-BAPTISTE

Most ImpactArise Publishing products are available at special quantity discounts for bulk purchase for sales promotions, premiums, fund-raising, and educational needs. For details, write ImpactArise Publishing, 2501 Chatham Road, Suite R, Springfield, Illinois 62704, email workbooks@arisetogrowkids.com, or call 708-740-7850.

Teen Bible Study Workbook - POWER: EDITION
by Regine Jean-Baptiste
Published by ImpactArise Publishing Company
2501 Chatham Road, Suite R
Springfield, Illinois 62704
www.arisetogrowkids.com

This book or parts thereof may not be reproduced in any form, stored in a retrieval system, or transmitted in any form by any means—electronic, mechanical, photocopy, recording, or otherwise—without prior written permission of the publisher, except as provided by United States of America copyright law.

Scripture quotations marked (TPT) The Passion Translation®. Copyright © 2017, 2018, 2020 by Passion & Fire Ministries, Inc. Used by permission. All rights reserved.

Scripture quotations marked (ESV) are taken from the ESV® Bible (The Holy Bible, English Standard Version®), copyright © 2001 by Crossway, a publishing ministry of Good News Publishers. Used by permission. All rights reserved.

Scripture quotations marked (NIV) are taken from the New International Version®, NIV®. Copyright © 1973, 1978, 1984, 2011 by Biblica, Inc.™ Used by permission of Zondervan. All rights reserved worldwide. www.zondervan.com The "NIV" and "New International Version" are trademarks registered in the United States Patent and Trademark Office by Biblica, Inc.™

Scripture quotations marked (NLT) are from the New Living Translation, copyright ©1996, 2004, 2015 by Tyndale House Foundation. Used by permission of Tyndale House Publishers, Carol Stream, Illinois 60188. All rights reserved

Clipart provided by Freepik from www.flaticon.com. Launching Activity, Key Takeaway, Activity, Daily Engagement icons made by Freepik. Teaching icon made by Gregor Cresnar. Book cover designed by coolvector / Freepik. Instagram png designed by Pugazh Productions from Pngtree. Multiple flower png designed by Pngtree. Give Thanks drawing © 2019 Crayola. Serpentine Design®
Copyright © 2022 by Regine Jean-Baptiste

All rights reserved.

Visit the Arise to Grow Kids website at arisetogrowkids.com

ISBN-13: 979-8-4365809-0-6
ISBN-10: 8-4365-8090-6

While the author has made every effort to provide accurate Internet addresses at the time of publication, neither the publisher nor the author assumes any responsibility for errors or for changes that occur after publication.

22 23 24 25 26 — 9 8 7 6 5 4 3 2 1

Printed in the United States of America.

*To all of the superheroes
in God's Kingdom...*

TABLE OF CONTENTS

Getting Started 3

Tenn Study Agreement 5

Lesson 1: Captain God 7

Lesson 2: Kingdom Power 17

Lesson 3: Turbo Charge Kingdom Power 31

Lesson 4: Kryptonite 49

Lesson 5: Power to Win 59

Lesson 6: A Powerful Life 71

About the Author 80

GETTING STARTED

The *Teen Bible Study Workbook* is filled with lessons to help you learn more about God. Put what you learn into practice, and you will experience God daily.

HOW TO USE THIS WORKBOOK

Each lesson is designed with the same structure:

WELCOME – Time to check-in and celebrate joys from the week.

OPENING PRAYER – Pause to rejoice and ask God to help us learn and experience the lesson.

FOCUS SCRIPTURE – Read the key Bible verse about our lesson topic.

LAUNCHING ACTIVITY – Discussion question to get us talking about the Scripture.

TEACHING – Answer to our lesson question.

ACTIVITY – Putting what we learned into action!

KEY TAKEAWAY – Summary of the lesson's important points.

DAILY ENGAGEMENT – Homework to help us apply what we learned.

TIPS FOR STUDY

Here are three tips to get more fun out of this workbook:

1. Read the instructions.

2. Think about the scriptures provided in each lesson.

3. Do the activities and homework to practice what you learn.

ADDITIONAL SUPPLIES NEEDED

- Bible. You can also read the Bible online at www.bible.com or if you have a cellphone download the Bible app.

- Pencil / Pen to take notes.

- Color Pencils / Crayons / Markers for when we get creative.

TEEN STUDY AGREEMENT

The *Teen Study Agreement* will help us learn about God, be safe in class, and have fun together!

- Be on time. Show up a few minutes before study time to be admitted into the class.
- Be Kind. All comments and discussions should be respectful.
- No other devices during class. Focus your attention on the study lesson.
- Treat others the way you want to be treated.
- Have fun!

    <u>*Virtual Study Only*</u>

    - Mute your microphone when you are not speaking.
    - Adjust your camera and lighting so we can see your face well.

ADDITIONAL HOUSE RULES

Did we forget anything? List any rules you would like for us to add to the agreement.

_____

Sign the agreement below:

I _____ understand and agree to the study rules listed above. I promise that I will try my best to live by these rules so that our Bible study time is fun and exciting place for everyone!

_____   _____
Name   *Date*

LESSON 1: CAPTAIN GOD

A new command I give you: Love one another.
As I have loved you, so you must love one another.
— John 13:34 NIV

👋 WELCOME: A NEW STORY

Complete the statement to share with your study group.

I'm here. Super _____ and

I'm ready to _____

_____

_____

_____ .

_____

💬 OPENING PRAYER

Let us pray...

📖 FOCUS SCRIPTURE

My beloved friends, let us continue to love each other since love comes from God. Everyone who loves is born of God and experiences a relationship with God. The person who refuses to love doesn't know the first thing about God, because God is love—so you can't know him if you don't love.

— *1 John 4:7–8 MSG*

🚀 LAUNCHING ACTIVITY: START AT LOVE

Answer the following question:

- **How would you define the word love?**

💡 TEACHING

Use the space below to write your lesson notes.

- **What is one word we can use to describe God?**

- **Why is it important for us to understand how God defines love?**

- **How can we see or experience God's love?**

ACTIVITY: LOVE IN ACTION!

The following questions will help you create a plan to experience God's love. Write your answers in the heart.

1. Fill in the three areas that define God's love.

2. Circle one area of God's love you want to connect with this week?

3. List one thing you will do this week to experience more of God's love in the area you circled.

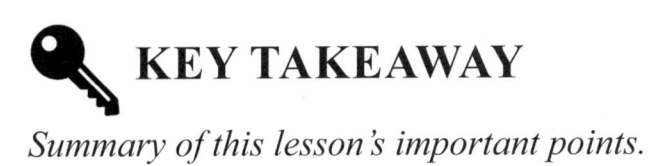

🔑 KEY TAKEAWAY

Summary of this lesson's important points.

_____ comes from God's love.

DAILY ENGAGEMENT

Homework to help us apply what we learned.

Study / Review the names of God cards.

- This week study/review the front and back of the names of God cards printed in your workbook. The front of each card has the names of God in the original language and English. When you flip the page, the back of the card is available. The back of the card gives you the definition of each name, more Scriptures where that name is found in the Bible, and a sentence of how this name for God shapes your identity.*

- Every day, place a check in the box next to the card you reviewed.

- Feel free to cut out the cards to use them as study cards.

*Need help saying the name of God in the original language? Visit the Names of God Playlist on YouTube using the following link for help: http:/bit.ly/GodsPowerName

Name of God Video

- Record your friendship story. In your video, share your story of how you became friends with Jesus. You can also share your favorite fact about Jesus. If you are posting online tag @arisetogrowkids for a repost

☐ Reviewed This Week

ELI MAELEKHI
God My King

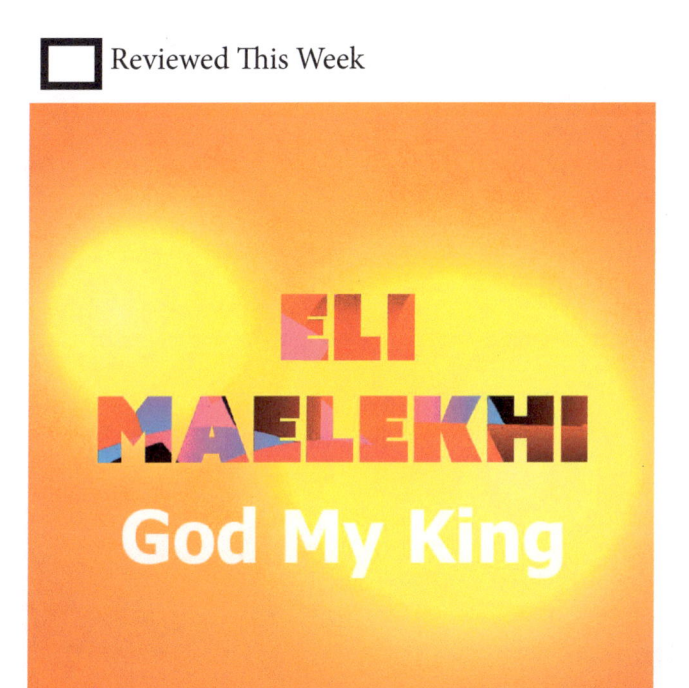

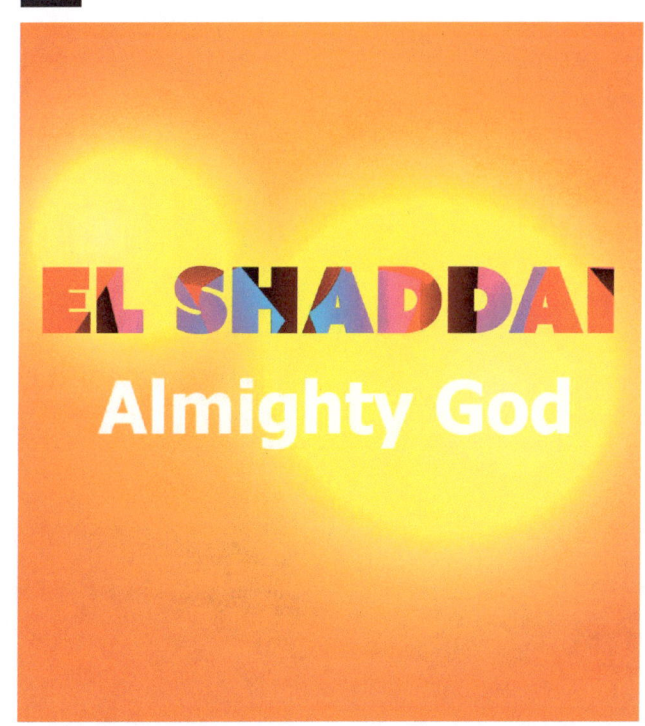

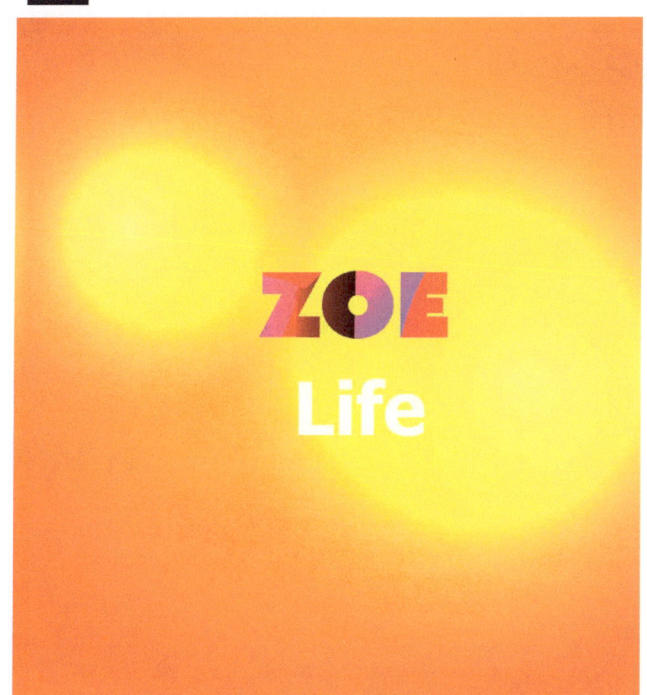

☐ Reviewed This Week

EL SHADDAI
Almighty God

☐ Reviewed This Week

ZOE
Life

☐ Reviewed This Week

MAON
Dwelling Place

El Shaddai | Almighty God
God's covenant-keeping love initiates and maintains His promises in my life; therefore; there is nothing impossible for me through God.

Key Scripture:
Genesis 17:1-2

Supporting Scriptures:
Psalm 91:1-2; Proverbs 18:10

Identity Affirmation:
I live in the impossible of God.
Everything is working for my good.

Eli Maelekhi | God My King
God's eternal Kingdom of peace and righteousness goes before me. The foundation of His throne is righteousness and justice; God's love and faithfulness goes before us.

Key Scriptures:
Psalm 68:24

Supporting Scriptures:
Psalms 24:7-10; 47:7

Identity Affirmation:
I am a child of the King (a princess/ a prince).

Maon | Dwelling Place
God is my refuge that dwells not just with me, but within my life.

Key Scripture:
Psalm 91:1-2

Supporting Scripture:
Ephesians 2:22

Identity Affirmation:
The Holy Spirit dwells within me.

Zóé | Life
Jesus comes to add to my life everything that God designed and purposed me to experience for the glory of His Name.

Key Scripture:
John 14:6

Supporting Scriptures:
John 10:10; Acts 3:15; Colossians 3:4; 1 John 1:1

Identity Affirmation:
I have abundant life in Christ!

☐ Reviewed This Week

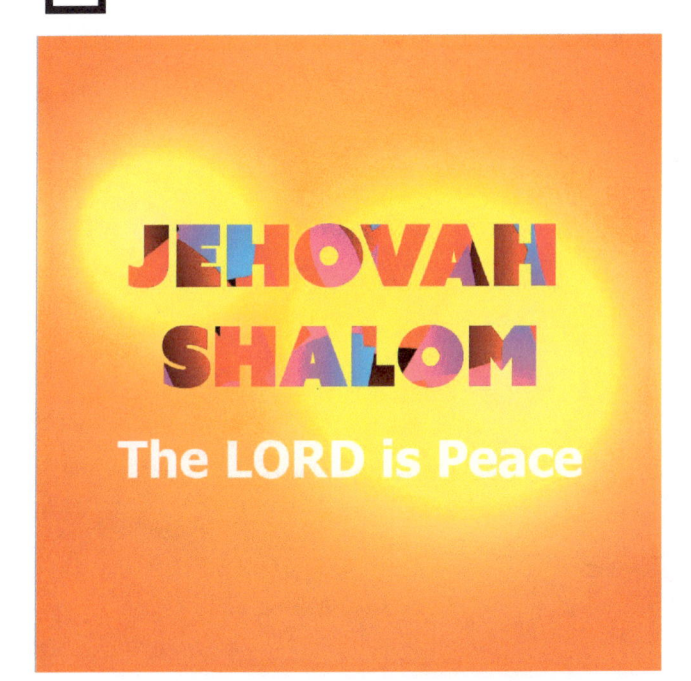

JEHOVAH SHALOM
The LORD is Peace

☐ Reviewed This Week

HODOS
Way

☐ Reviewed This Week

JEHOVAH EL EMETH
LORD God of Truth

Hodos | Way
Jesus provides clear direction for every destination God calls me to reach.

Key Scripture:
John 14:6

Supporting Scriptures:
John 11:16; 20:24-29

Identity Affirmation:
I have clarity of heart, mind, and direction at all times in my life through Jesus Christ.

Jehovah Shalom | The LORD is Peace
God causes me to live in harmony with Him and others. He expresses His faithfulness to me in wholeness, inner calmness, and makes me to live in absence of outward conflict.

Key Scripture:
Judges 6:24

Supporting Scriptures:
Proverbs 3:13, 17; Isaiah 26:3; Galatians 5:22; Philippians 4:6-7

Identity Affirmation:
I will live in peace.

Jehovah El Emeth | LORD God of Truth
God's truth found in Jesus Christ, who is the Word of God, brings life.

Key Scripture:
Psalm 31:5

Supporting Scripture:
John 14:6

Identity Affirmation:
I am a truth-teller!

LESSON 2: KINGDOM POWER

For the Kingdom of God is not just a lot of talk; it is living by God's power.

— 1 Corinthians 4:20 NLT

👏 WELCOME: GROUP PIC

Draw a picture of yourself with some of your favorite people inside the picture frame.

💬 OPENING PRAYER

Let us pray...

📖 FOCUS SCRIPTURE

And now, because we are united to Christ, we both have equal and direct access in the realm of the Holy Spirit to come before the Father!

— *Ephesians 2:18 TPT*

🚀 LAUNCHING ACTIVITY: SQUAD GOALS

What are some commonalities between you and your squad? List them in the chart below:

Things I have in common with my family...	Things I have in common with my friends...	Things I have in common with my classmates at school...	Things I have in common with my Bible Study group ...

💡 TEACHING

Use the space below to write your lesson notes.

- **What are commonalities among friends of God?**

- **How do we access the power of God?**

- **P. R. A. Y. Method**

    1. P:

    2. R:

    3. A:

4. Y:

- Senses:

- Pictures:

- Thoughts:

- Others:

- Scripture:

- Environment:

In Jesus Christ name, I pray. Amen.

- **How should friends of Jesus use their power?**

⟳ ACTIVITY: HEARING TEST

Rate each of the following statements using the scale:

(1) Not me

(3) Sometimes like me

(5) That's ME all the time!

(1) _____ I often think of something someone will say or do before they say or do it.

(2) _____ Strangers or friends often say something unknowingly that helps me make a decision.

(3) _____ I often have dreams when I sleep or see pictures when I close my eyes.

(4) _____ When I am outside playing or taking a walk, I often get solutions to my questions.

(5) _____ I often get solutions to my questions when I read my Bible.

(6) _____ I can often feel when something good or bad is going to happen.

- *Match your highest scoring statement(s) to the corresponding number in the Gifts to Yield list.*

Types of Gifts to Yield

1. Thoughts - Wise thoughts from God.

2. Others - God's love speak to me through others.

3. Pictures - Picture communication from God.

4. Environment - God's wisdom comes through nature and the things around me.

5. Scripture - Bible inspiration from God.

6. Senses - Communication through sight, sound, smell, taste, or touch.

- *Write your answers below. Your primary way of hearing God's voice is your highest scoring statement(s). Your secondary way of hearing God's voice is your second highest scoring statement(s).*

My Gift to Hear God!

- **My primary way to hear God is** _____

- **My secondary way to hear God is** _____
_____

🔑 KEY TAKEAWAY

Summary of this lesson's important point.

_____ of Jesus have the power to love _____,

_____, and others. We grow in love by _____

and _____ to God.

📓 DAILY ENGAGEMENT

Homework to help us apply what we learned.

Exercise Your Ear

- Practice hearing the voice of God.

    1. Pick a question.

    2. Spend some time in prayer, talking and listening to God's answer to question prompt.

    3. Journal about your communication with God. Share any additional reflections or feelings about your experience.

Ask God what He loves most about you. List all the thoughts or pictures you see below:

_____

_____

_____

_____

_____

_____

_____

_____

_____

_____

Read Ephesians 2:18 TPT and ask God to highlight words in this Scripture that can encourage you. List the word(s) in the scripture that inspires you.

Don't be afraid, for I am with you. Don't be discouraged, for I am your God. I will strengthen you and help you. I will hold you up with my victorious right hand.
— *Isaiah 41:10 NLT*

_____

_____

_____

_____

_____

_____

_____

_____

_____

Ask God what is one thing you did last week that made Him smile. List any thoughts or pictures below:

_____

_____

_____

_____

_____

_____

_____

_____

_____

_____

_____

Ask God to show you a picture of something He loves about your parent(s). List any thoughts or pictures below:

_____

_____

_____

_____

_____

_____

_____

_____

_____

_____

Ask God to share with you something He likes to smell. When you are inside or outside, take a deep breath. What do you smell? List any thoughts or pictures below:

_____

_____

_____

_____

_____

_____

_____

_____

_____

_____

P.R.A.Y.

P. PAUSE

R. REJOICE

A. ASK

Y. YIELD

LESSON 3: TURBO CHARGE KINGDOM POWER

*Yahweh has established his throne in heaven;
his kingdom rules the entire universe.*
— *Psalm 103:19 TPT*

👋 WELCOME: BLOOMING GARDEN

- *On the blue flowers, list three things you started doing with help but, have grown to do on your own.*
- *On the yellow flowers, list three things you hope to one day grow and do on your own.*

💬 OPENING PRAYER

Let us pray...

But grow in the grace and knowledge of our Lord and Savior Jesus Christ.
To him be glory both now and forever! Amen.
— *2 Peter 3:18 NIV*

- **P. Pause to think of the name of God:**

- **R: Rejoice in the promise:**

- **A: Ask:**

- **Y. Yield:**

In Jesus Christ name, I pray. Amen.

FOCUS SCRIPTURE

But seek first the kingdom of God and his righteousness, and all these things will be added to you.

— *Matthew 6:33 ESV*

LAUNCHING ACTIVITY: GROWTH CHART

Complete the chart. List some of the ways that growth happens:

How humans physically grow...	How plants physically grow...	How animals physically grow...	How rivers or lakes grow...

- Besides physical growth, what are some other areas in our lives that require growth and development?

- Review your list of the ways people can develop their lives. Which of these areas of growth are most important?

TEACHING

Use the space below to write your lesson notes.

- **How can we increase our power?**

- **Why does God want us to have power?**

- **Why is it important to grow spiritually?**

ACTIVITY: FIRST THINGS IS FIRST!

Identify your priority for growth.

- **Review the *First Things First* cards.***

- **Select your top five priorities. Rank their importance in your life using the following scale:**

    (1) Very Important

    (2) Mostly Important

    (3) Important

    (4) Slightly Important

    (5) Not at all important

    Feel free to cut out the cards for this activity.

- **List your top priorities for growth. You can also paste your cards below.**

FAMILY	SCHOOL
GOD	PLAYTIME

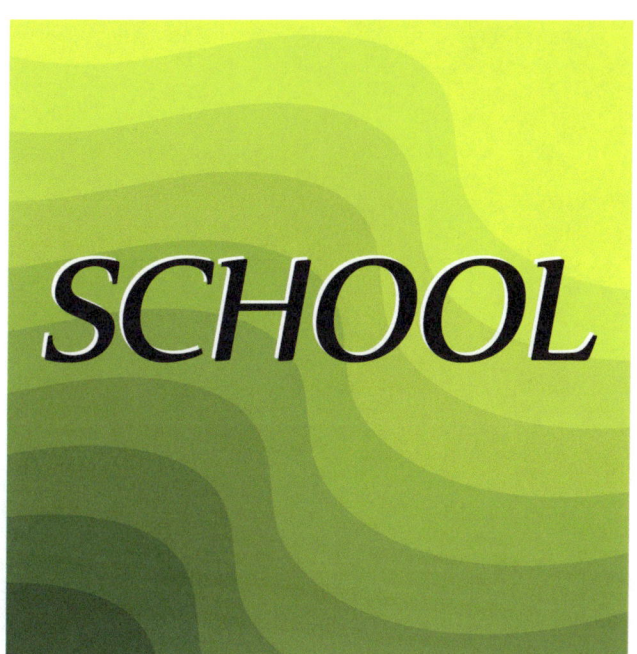

SCHOOL	FAMILY
PLAYTIME	GOD

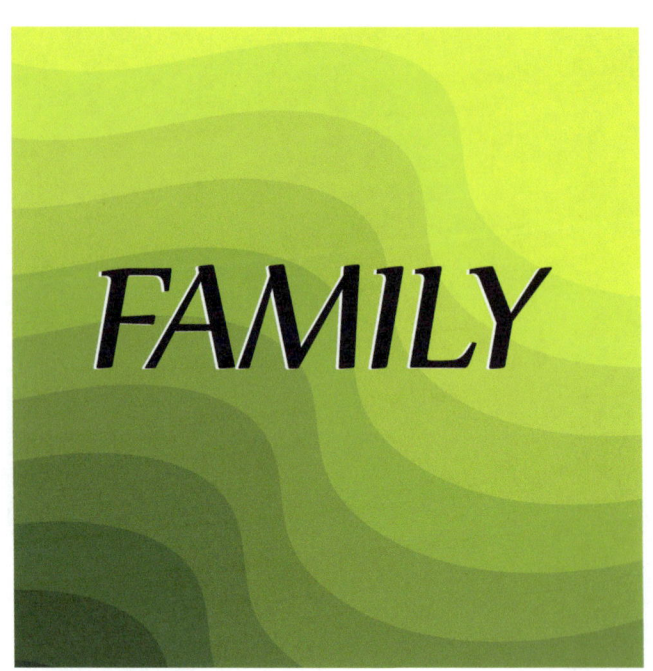

ME	FRIENDS
REST / SLEEP	HONESTY

FRIENDS	ME
HONESTY	REST / SLEEP

COURAGE	RESPECT
REWARDS OR GIFTS	HAPPINESS

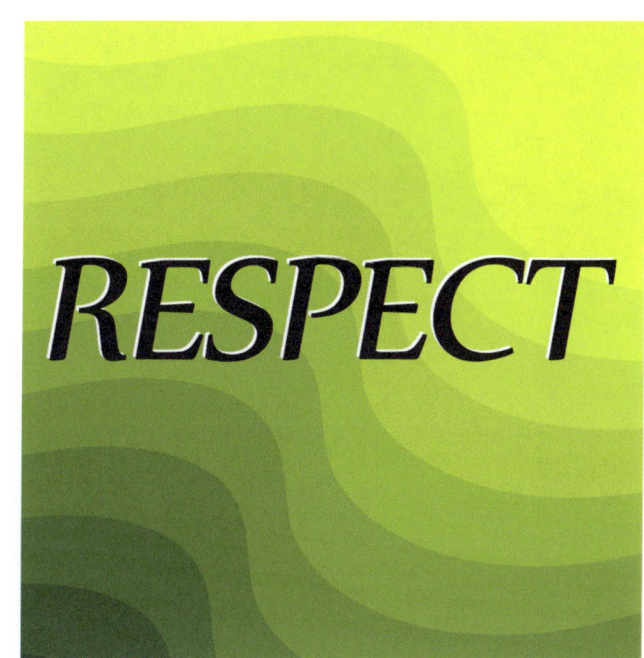

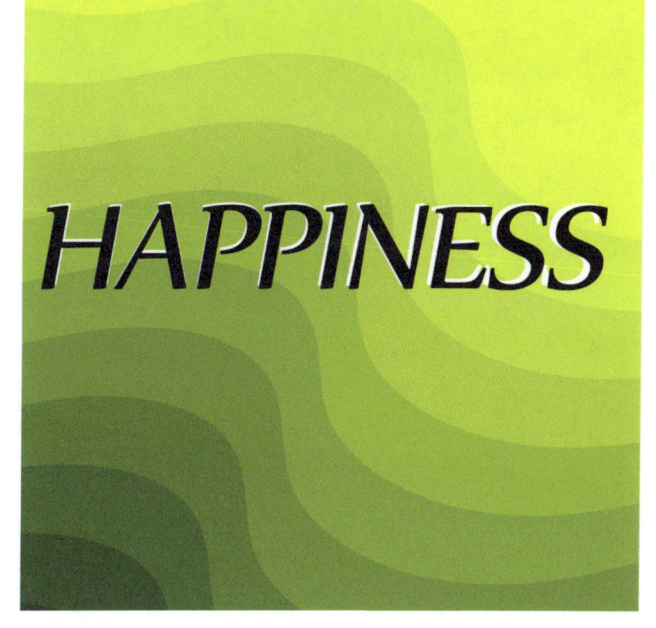

RESPECT	COURAGE
HAPPINESS	REWARDS OR GIFTS

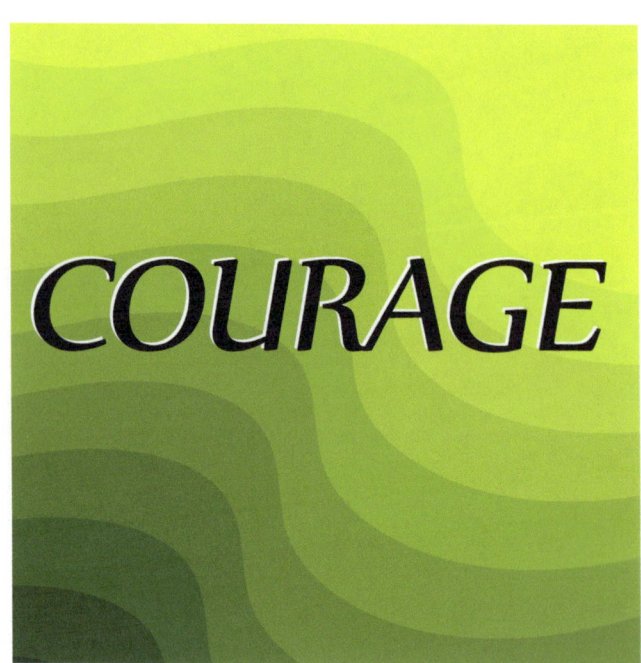

- **Here is how God asks us to prioritize our lives:**

Bible answer:

You are to love the Lord Yahweh, your God, with a passionate heart, from the depths of your soul, with your every thought, and with all your strength. This is the great and supreme commandment. And the second is this: 'You must love your neighbor in the same way you love yourself.' You will never find a greater commandment than these."

— *Mark 12:30-31 TPT*

(1) Very Important *(2)* Important *(3)* Important

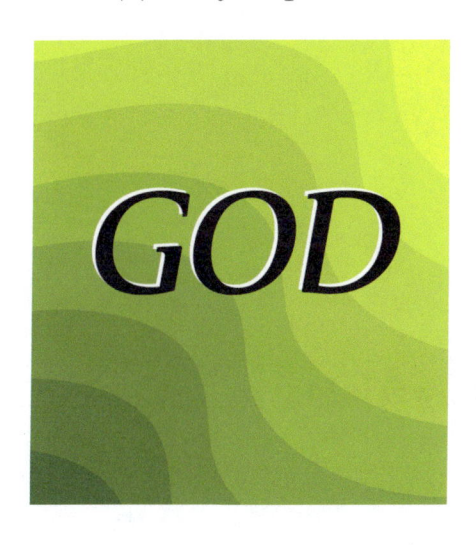

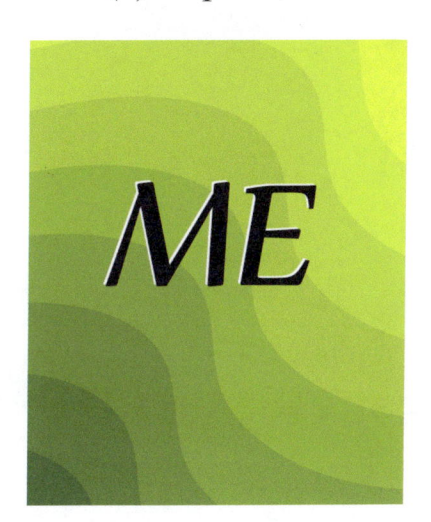

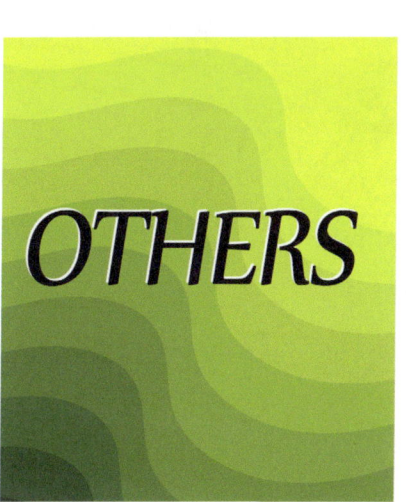

GOD **ME** **OTHERS**

- **How does God's list of prioritizes differ from your list? How are these list similar?**

- **What are some ways we can remember to put God first?**

🔑 KEY TAKEAWAY

Summary of this lesson's important point.

We _____ in the power of love

by making God our number _____ priority!

DAILY ENGAGEMENT

Homework to help us apply what we learned.

Report Card

- Practice prioritizing God this week by using prayer. Speak and listen to God throughout the day. In your prayer time ask, "God, what is next?" Then listen to His response, report any thoughts or pictures, and document the results of your actions in the journal below.

Weekly Report

- **Report for Day 1: "God, what is next?"**

Notes/Comments

- **Report for Day 2: "God, what is next?"**

Notes/Comments

- **Report for Day 3: "God, what is next?"**

Notes/Comments

- **Report for Day 4: "God, what is next?"**

Notes/Comments

- **Report for Day 5: "God, what is next?"**

Notes/Comments

- **Report for Day 6: "God, what is next?"**

Notes/Comments

- **Report for Day 7: "God, what is next?"**

Notes/Comments

LESSON 4: KRYPTONITE

For God will never give you the spirit of fear, but the Holy Spirit who gives you mighty power, love, and self-control.

—2 Timothy 1:7 TPT

WELCOME: BATTERY CHECK

Color the battery to the line that represents how you are feeling today. The battery goes from - =not feeling great at all to + = feeling the best I've ever felt.

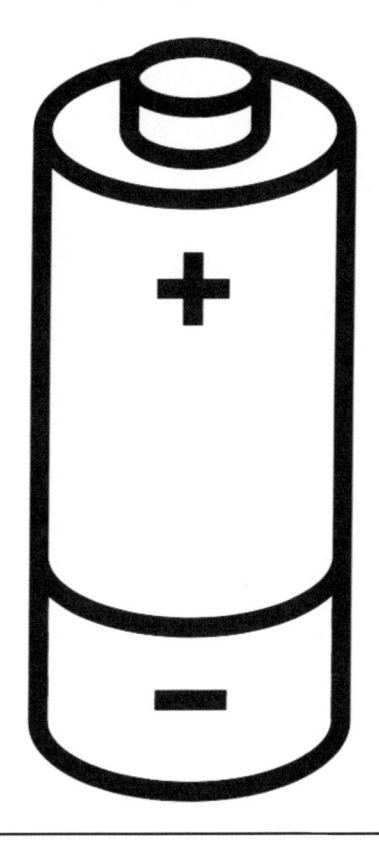

💬 OPENING PRAYER

Let us pray...

> *Revive us again, O God! I know you will! Give us a fresh start! Then all your people will taste your joy and gladnesss.*

> — *Psalm 85:6 TPT*

- **P. Pause to think of the name of God:** O, God!

- **R: Rejoice in the promise:**

- **A: Ask:**

- **Y. Yield:**

In Jesus' name, I pray. Amen.

FOCUS SCRIPTURE

There is no fear in love. But perfect love drives out fear, because fear has to do with punishment. The one who fears is not made perfect in love.

— Psalm 1 John 4:18 NIV

LAUNCHING ACTIVITY: POWER DRAIN

Answer the following question:

- **What are some activities or situations that cause you to be sad, have a lack of energy, or feel tired?**

💡 TEACHING

Use the space below to write your lesson notes.

- **What is a barrier to seeing God's power in our lives?**

- **What are things that drain our God-given power?**

- **How do we recognize these roadblocks to the power of God's love?**

Fear looks like...	Distrust looks like...	Hate looks like...

ACTIVITY: LIVE VICTORIOUSLY

What are some things you can do when fear, distrust, and hate come to weaken your power to love God, yourself, and others? List possible solutions in the chart below:

My plan against fear...	My plan against distrust...	My plan against hate...

KEY TAKEAWAY

Summary of this lesson's important points.

_____, _____ and _____

fight against the power of God's love!

DAILY ENGAGEMENT

Homework to help us apply what we learned.

Battery Inspector

- This week keep an eye out to see if roadblocks show up to drain your power to love God, self, or others. Record any roadblocks you experienced to share with the study group.

Inspector Report

- **Battery Drain Report for Day 1:**

Notes/Comments

- **Battery Drain Report for Day 2:**

Notes/Comments

- **Battery Drain Report for Day 3:**

Notes/Comments

- **Battery Drain Report for Day 4:**

Notes/Comments

- **Battery Drain Report for Day 5:**

Notes/Comments

Turbo Charge Your Power

- *Defend against the barriers to God's love by building up your identity. Review / Study the I AM card. Place a check in the box after you have reviewed each card.*

☐ Reviewed This Week

I AM WONDERFUL

☐ Reviewed This Week

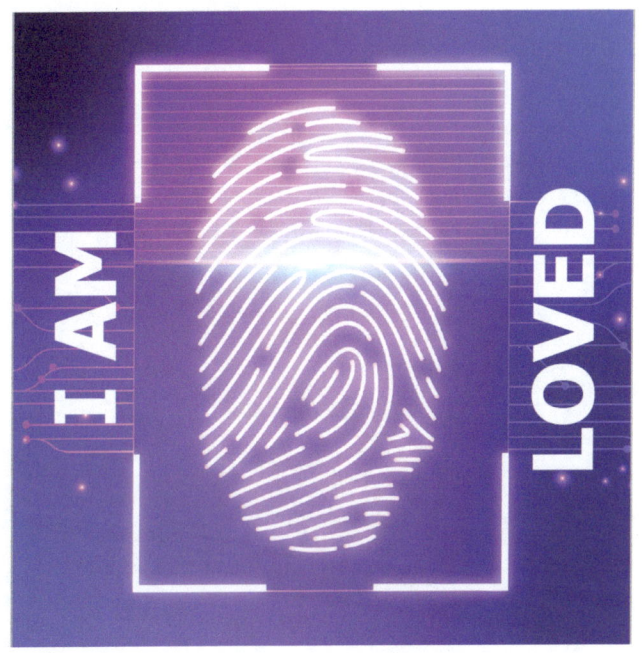

I AM LOVED

☐ Reviewed This Week

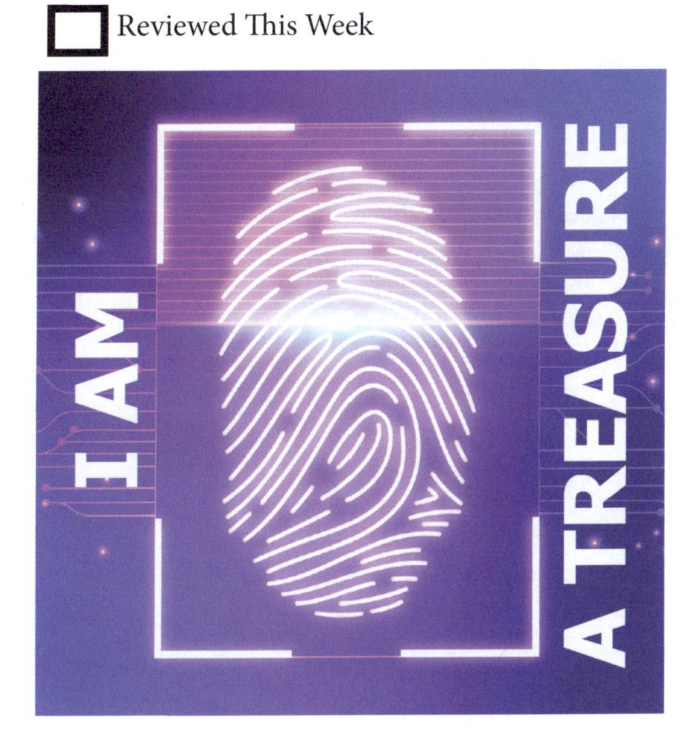

I AM A TREASURE

☐ Reviewed This Week

I AM BLESSED

☐ Reviewed This Week

I Am Loved

This is love: He loved us long before we loved him. It was his love, not ours. He proved it by sending his Son to be the pleasing sacrificial offering to take away our sins.
— 1 John 4:10 TPT

Identity Affirmation:
I am loved by God. God proves His love for me in Christ Jesus.

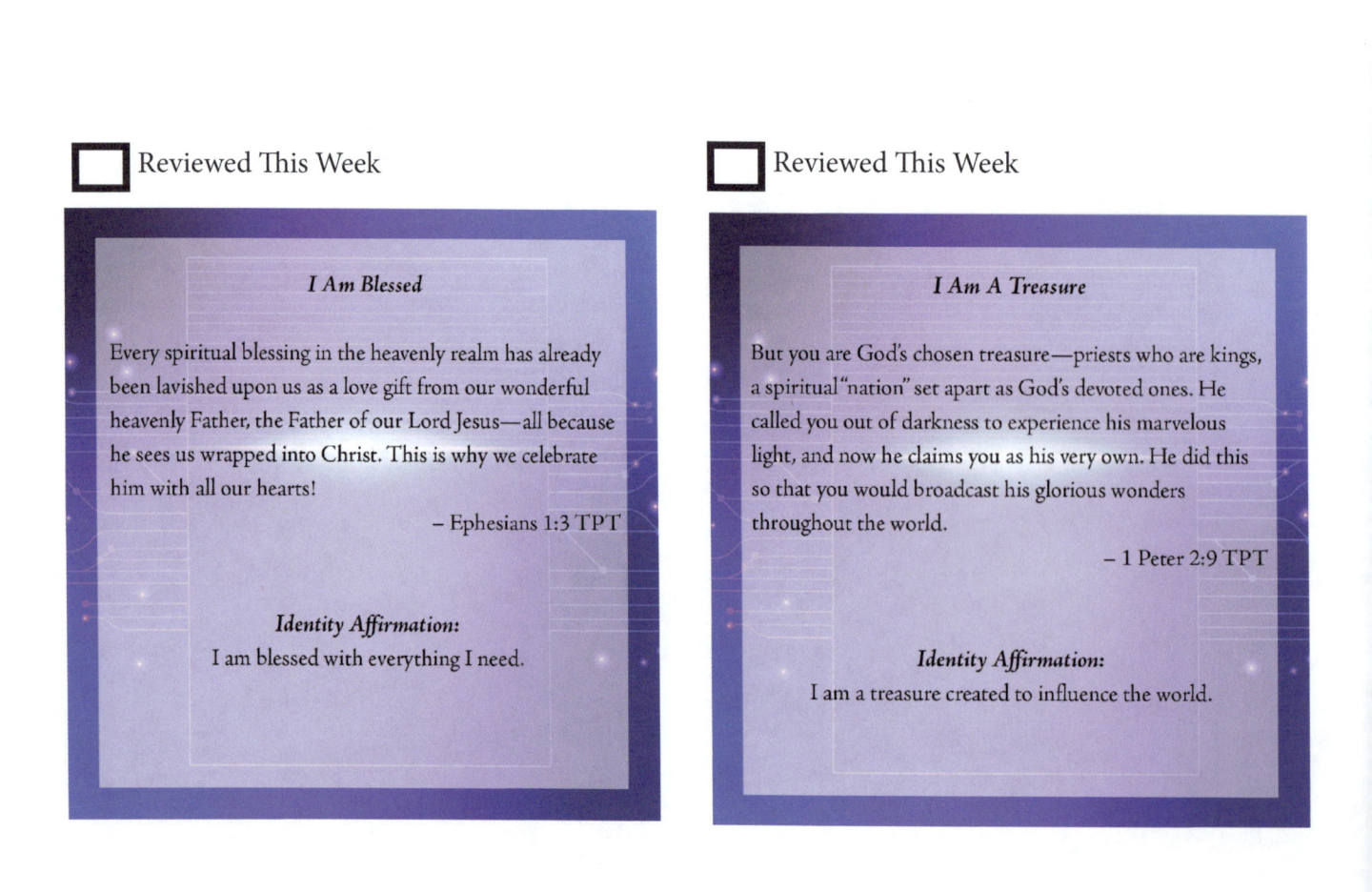

☐ Reviewed This Week

I Am Wonderful

I praise you, for I am fearfully and wonderfully made. Wonderful are your works; my soul knows it very well.
— Psalm 139:14 ESV

Identity Affirmation:
I am mysteriously complex and, yet, a marvelously breathtaking creation of God.

☐ Reviewed This Week

I Am Blessed

Every spiritual blessing in the heavenly realm has already been lavished upon us as a love gift from our wonderful heavenly Father, the Father of our Lord Jesus—all because he sees us wrapped into Christ. This is why we celebrate him with all our hearts!
— Ephesians 1:3 TPT

Identity Affirmation:
I am blessed with everything I need.

☐ Reviewed This Week

I Am A Treasure

But you are God's chosen treasure—priests who are kings, a spiritual "nation" set apart as God's devoted ones. He called you out of darkness to experience his marvelous light, and now he claims you as his very own. He did this so that you would broadcast his glorious wonders throughout the world.
— 1 Peter 2:9 TPT

Identity Affirmation:
I am a treasure created to influence the world.

LESSON 5: POWER TO WIN

There is no power above us or beneath us—no power that could ever be found in the universe that can distance us from God's passionate love, which is lavished upon us through our Lord Jesus, the Anointed One!

— Romans 8:39 TPT

WELCOME: HIGHLIGHT THE POSITIVE

List three sunny moments you experienced this week that brought you joy.

💬 OPENING PRAYER

Let us pray...

Yahweh, you are my soul's celebration. How could I ever forget the miracles of kindness you've done for me?

— *Psalms 103:2 TPT*

- **P. Pause to think of the name of God:** Yahweh...

- **R: Rejoice in the promise:**

- **A: Ask:**

- **Y. Yield:**

In Jesus' name, I pray. Amen.

FOCUS SCRIPTURE

Love the Lord your God with all your heart and with all your soul and with all your strength.

— *Deuteronomy 6:5 NIV*

LAUNCHING ACTIVITY: SETTING THE STANDARD

Answer the following questions:

- **What are some guidelines/rules from home or school that help protect and guide your actions?**

- **Why are rules helpful?**

💡 TEACHING

Use the space below to write your lesson notes.

- **What is God's standard?**

- **What is sin?**

- **How does sin affect our superpowers?**

- **How do we remove sin and its consequences to refill our power tank?**

- **What is our prayer shield and how does it help?**

1. *Lordship Prayer:*

2. *Repentance Prayer:*

3. *Forgiveness Prayer:*

4. *Release Prayer:*

5. *Remove Prayer:*

ACTIVITY: REMOVING BARRIERS TO LOVE

Spend time talking to God. Pray and ask God to remove any barriers working against your power to love God, ourselves, and others.

1. **Lordship Prayer:** *What do you like most about God?*

2. **Repentance Prayer:** *List any ways you may have missed God's standard.*

3. **Forgiveness Prayer:** *List anyone you want to forgive.*

4. **Release Prayer:** *Circle the prayer that applies to you.*

    - I don't hold what _____ did against me.

    - Thank you that once I say I am sorry God, you don't hold anything against me because of my friendship with Jesus.

5. **Remove Prayer:** *Write thanksgiving to God and list any request.*

🔑 KEY TAKEAWAY

Summary of this lesson's important point.

I have the _____ to overcome

_____ that fights God's love in my life.

Please share the following note with your parent(s) / guardian.

📓 DAILY ENGAGEMENT

Homework to help us apply what we learned.

Reconnect with Love!

- This week when you P.R.A.Y, be sure to use our prayer shield to remove anyways you have missed God's standard.

Prayer Shield to Fight Barriers & Win Aginist Evil!

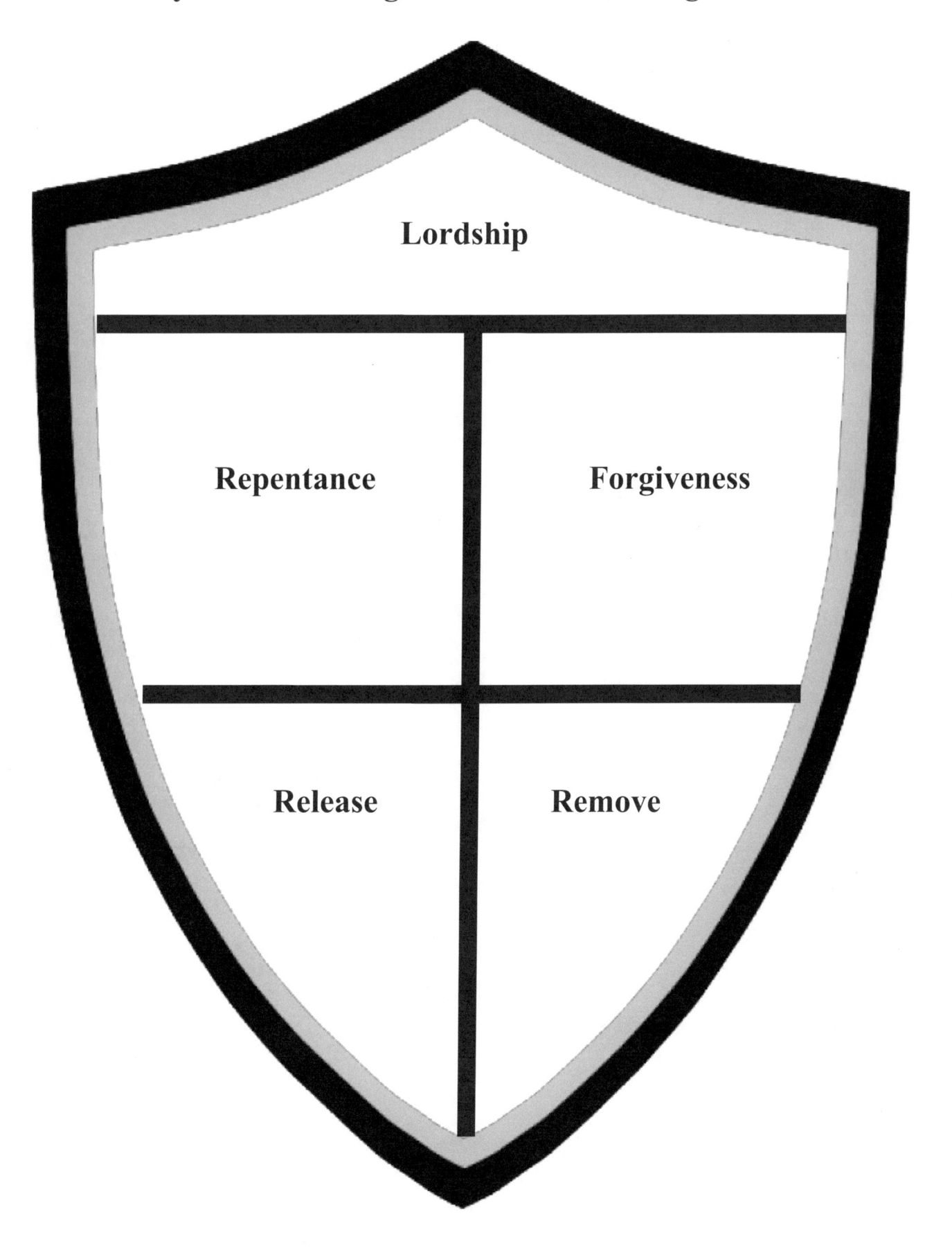

Lordship

Repentance

Forgiveness

Release

Remove

I Am Cards

- Reconnect with love by also studying more about your identity with the I AM cards.

Record any notes/comments from your study time.

☐ Reviewed This Week

I AM GIFTED

☐ Reviewed This Week

I AM A FRIEND

☐ Reviewed This Week

I AM AMAZING

☐ Reviewed This Week

I Am A Friend

No longer do I call you servants, for the servant does not know what his master is doing; but I have called you friends, for all that I have heard from my Father I have made known to you.

— John 15:15 ESV

Identity Affirmation:
I am a friend of Christ.

☐ Reviewed This Week

I Am Gifted

Every believer has received grace gifts, so use them to serve one another as faithful stewards of the many-colored tapestry of God's grace.

— 1 Peter 4:10 TPT

Identity Affirmation:
I am equipped by God with unique talents and skills to serve others. My abilities will render glory to God.

☐ Reviewed This Week

I Am Amazing

But God's amazing grace has made me who I am! And his grace to me was not fruitless. In fact, I worked harder than all the rest, yet not in my own strength but God's, for his empowering grace is poured out upon me.

— 1 Corinthians 15:10 TPT

Identity Affirmation:
I am not the great "I AM",
but by the grace of God, I am who I am.

LESSON 6: A POWERFUL LIFE

For I'm trained in the secret of overcoming all things, whether in fullness or in hunger. And I find that the strength of Christ's explosive power infuses me to conquer every difficulty.

— *Philippians 4:12b-13 TPT*

WELCOME: BEST THING EVER!

What are three things you are thankful for learning in this class.

1.

2.

3.

💬 OPENING PRAYER

Let us pray...

God can do anything, you know—far more than you could ever imagine or guess or request in your wildest dreams!

— *Ephesians 3:20 MSG*

- **P. Pause to think of the name of God:** God of my wildest dreams...

- **R: Rejoice in the promise:**

- **A: Ask:**

- **Y. Yield:**

In Jesus Christ name, I pray. Amen.

FOCUS SCRIPTURE

With this in mind, we constantly pray that our God will empower you to live worthy of all that he has invited you to experience. And we pray that by his power all the pleasures of goodness and all works inspired by faith would fill you completely.

— 2 Thessalonians 1:11 TPT

LAUNCHING ACTIVITY: CONNECT AGAIN

Answer the following question:

1. What are some ways you can reconnect with someone you haven't talked to in a long time?

💡 TEACHING

Use the space below to write your lesson notes.

- **What does it mean to live a powerful life?**

- **How do we live a powerful life full of God's love?**

- **Why is it important to live in the power of God's love?**

ACTIVITY: INSPIRATION STATION

Answer the following question:

- **How can we inspire others to love God, themselves, and others?**

🔑 KEY TAKEAWAY

Summary of this lesson's important point.

Staying _____ with God,

helps me to live a _____ life!

📓 DAILY ENGAGEMENT: THE JOURNEY CONTINUES

Homework to help us apply what we learned.

Video Verse

- Pick your favorite verse used in the *Kids Bible Study Workbook* to record a video verse. A video verse is a 30 second – 3-minute video that shares your verse and explains how you think the verse answers a specific question. The question for this week's video verse is: **Why is this your favorite verse?**

Here are some tips.

1. Feel free to do a video verse daily, each with a different scripture verse from our study.

2. Shy or feel like you don't know how to start your video verse? There is a script below with blanks to help you get started.

3. The video recording doesn't have to be perfect. Have fun!

Video Verse Script

Hello! My name is _____ *(first name only)* and welcome to video verse. We have key Bible verses that every kid should know.

Today's verse is_____.

This verse is my favorite because _____

_____

_____.

© 2019 Crayola. Serpentine Design®

Find everything imaginable at Crayola.com

ABOUT THE AUTHOR

Regine Jean-Baptiste is the founder of Arise to Grow (www.arisetogrow.com), an online community for adults and kids seeking to discover, develop and demonstrate faith. She has pastored in the United Methodist Church, overseen the Christian education department for a non-denominational church, and served as an Adjunct Professor of Religion and Philosophy at Saint Xavier University. Regine is passionate about helping people press forward to realize the fullness of their God-given destiny and purpose, as disciples of Jesus Christ. She holds a Masters of Divinity from Duke University. Regine currently resides in Chicago, IL.